DATE DUE

OCT 2 0 1998	
FEB 0 3 2000	

CHILDREN OF POVERTY

STUDIES ON THE EFFECTS
OF SINGLE PARENTHOOD,
THE FEMINIZATION OF POVERTY,
AND HOMELESSNESS

edited by

STUART BRUCHEY
UNIVERSITY OF MAINE

A GARLAND SERIES

ADOLESCENT RUNAWAY BEHAVIOR

WHO RUNS AND WHY

MICHAEL E. ROHR

GARLAND PUBLISHING, INC.
NEW YORK & LONDON / 1997

Library of Congress Cataloging-in-Publication Data

Rohr, Michael E., 1950–
    Adolescent runaway behavior : who runs and why / Michael
E. Rohr.
        p.   cm. — (Children of poverty)
    Includes bibliographical references and index.
    ISBN 0-8153-2292-5 (alk. paper)
    1. Personality Inventory for Children. 2. Runaway teenag-
ers—Psychological testing. I. Title. II. Series.
BF698.8.P47R64 1997
305.9'06923—dc21

                                            96-49246

Printed on acid-free, 250-year-life paper
Manufactured in the United States of America

This book is dedicated to

DICK JAMES

who has had faith in me for 11 years

A very special thanks to those who shared his faith

and especially to Gina

Contents

APPENDICES

Tables

Figures

Acknowledgments

A deep appreciation is extended to George Relyea of Computer Services at Memphis State University for the honor of experiencing his competence. I have learned from you.

A special thank you is extended to Cora Campbell for the formatting and final preparation of the work. Thank you very much.

Adolescent Runaway
Behavior

I

Introduction

This chapter provides an overview of the incidence of adolescent runaway behavior. In addition, problems associated with runaway behavior are discussed. Follow-up studies are reviewed and a need for the study is also established. The purpose of the study, research questions, hypotheses, definition of terms, assumptions, and limitations of the study conclude the chapter.

INCIDENCE

The phenomenon of adolescent runaway behavior has become a social and psychological problem of significant proportion. Runaway behavior is a social problem affecting a large segment of the nation's adolescent youth. Walker's (1975) review of the literature indicated that 1.5 percent to 2.7 percent of youth aged ten to seventeen had run away from home the previous year. The researchers that Walker (1975) reviewed were using 1970 and 1972 census data indicating that approximately five hundred thousand to one million teenagers had run away from home. Since Walker's review, estimates of runaway behavior have ranged from 1.3 million (Satchell, 1986) to 2 million (Freudenberger & Torkelsen, 1984) with predictions as high as 4 million runaways each year (The National Network of Runaway and Youth Services, 1985). Garbarino (1986) found that three percent of American families had a runaway youth each year.

The literature on the incidents of runaway behavior has focused on the relationship between the runaway and his or her family. A current review of the literature indicates that there are additional problematic areas of focus concerning the adolescent runaway. There are, in addition to the family related problems, parental problems, delinquent behavior, academic problems, peer relationship problems, and problems symptomatic of psychopathology.

PROBLEMS ASSOCIATED WITH ADOLESCENT
RUNAWAY BEHAVIOR

Family relationships. A relatively high incidence of runaway behavior
may be indicative of family discord. Blood and D'Angelo (1974) found
that adolescent runaways believed their homes were conflictual and
intolerable. The home may have been disrupted due to a family death,
parental divorce or separation (Ackerman, 1980). Johnson and Peck
(1978) indicated that the runaway had sibling rivalry problems. Gullotta
(1979) found that there were communication problems within the home
and that the runaways had feelings of being unwanted and rejected by
their parents (Adler, 1980).

Parental problems. The parents of adolescent runaways experienced
problems of their own. Brandon (1975) found that the parents in his study
tended to use excessive punishment. In his sample of runaways Steinbock
(1978) found that their parents had a history of drug use.

Delinquent behavior. Maar (1984) determined that runaway
adolescents themselves had alcohol and drug problems while Linden
(1979) found that adolescent runaways may be adjudicated delinquents.
The adolescent runaway may have stolen outside the home (Edelbrock,
1980); been defiant (Riemer, 1940); and disobeyed parental rules (Blood
and D'Angelo, 1974). Nye (1980) found in his sample that the adolescent
runaway had a history of truancy.

School problems. In addition to the runaway being truant from school,
Nye (1980) found that the runaway had a negative attitude toward school.
Gutierres and Reich (1981) identified the adolescent runaway as having
school behavior problems. Roberts (1982a) found that runaways had poor
problem-solving skills.

Peer relationships. Social competence has also been identified in the
literature as problematic for adolescent runaways. Gilchrist (1984)
reported that the adolescent runaway had poor social relationships and
Gullotta (1979) found that runaways had problems communicating with
members of their own family.

Symptoms of psychopathology. Some of the above reviewed research
indicated that the behaviors associated with the adolescent runaway may
be symptomatic of adolescent psychopathology (APA, 1987). Those
behaviors were stealing outside the home (Edelbrock, 1980), truancy

(Nye, 1980), disobeying parental rules (Blood & D'Angelo, 1974), and being adjudicated delinquent (Linden, 1979).

Other researchers have also found factors associated with the adolescent runaway that may be symptomatic of adolescent psychopathology. Those factors were anxiety (Williams, 1977); suicidal tendencies (Norey & Donahue, 1985); physical abuse (Harris, 1980); and sexual abuse (Hughes, 1981).

The results of the National Network of Runaway Youth Services (NNRYS, 1985) survey seem to support some of the above research findings. The NNRYS surveyed approximately 50,000 youth in runaway facilities and found that some of the presenting problems were depression, suicidal tendencies, alcohol and drug problems, physical abuse, sexual abuse, and the generic category - severe psychological problems.

FOLLOW-UP STUDIES

To assess the impact of running away upon the adolescent, longitudinal studies have been conducted. Follow-up studies on former runaways indicated that they did not adjust well to the demands of life. Earlier work, such as that of Robins (1958), found that former runaways had higher rates of mental illness--specifically sociopathic personality. Robins and O'Neal (1959) found that former runaways had more frequent arrests and divorces than non-runaways. Later studies indicated that runaways curtailed their schooling, had trouble with the law (Olson, 1977), and required the assistance of social service agencies for nervous and emotional troubles (Olson, Liebow, Mannino, & Shore, 1980).

METHODOLOGICAL CRITICISMS

Critical reviews of the research literature on runaways indicate methodological problems. Walker's (1975) review of the existing literature on runaway behavior revealed 156 citations of which 82 were professional journal articles and dissertations. In her critique, she concluded that the usefulness of these existing studies was limited due to their varying methodologies, designs, and assumptions. Specifically, with regard to the classification and typological systems of runaway behavior, none of these studies reflected a conceptual framework broad enough to encompass the range of behaviors associated with runaways. The methodologies were poor, the samples inappropriate, and the designs were typically inadequate to draw sound scientific conclusions.

A review of the literature from 1975 to 1988 indicated an increase in research interest on runaways. At least two hundred fifty eight professional journal articles and dissertations had been published during that time span. However, of those studies, very few responded well to the above-mentioned methodological and design criticisms by Walker (1975).

Adams and Munro (1979) reviewed the available literature on the psychopathology of runaway behavior and concluded that due to methodological problems with the research, the psychological factors associated with running away were either antecedent to or consequences of running away. Adams and Munro (1979) stated " ... we cannot be assured that psychological profiles are adequate predictors of runaway behavior or consequences of such action" (p. 361).

NEED FOR THE STUDY

The research literature indicates that the number of actual and potential runaways, along with their presenting problems and personality characteristics, would seem to necessitate a method for identifying potential adolescent runaways and their behaviors. What seems to be needed is first, evidence of an assessment instrument that is representative of the range of behavior problems runaway adolescents experience; second, indicators that this instrument might accurately determine a cluster of behaviors or profile associated with adolescent runaway behavior and third, based upon this profile, evidence that runaways can be distinguished from non-runaway criterion groups.

ADOLESCENT RUNAWAY PROFILE

Syndrome. The research indicates that the behaviors associated with adolescent runaways have not been presented as a cluster of identifying behaviors. There does not seem to be a research agenda which focuses on systematically and empirically exploring the adolescent runaway phenomena. The first indication of a profile of adolescent behavior that was representative of the empirical relationships found in the literature was provided by a survey conducted by the National Network of Runaway and Youth Services (1985). This survey found that the most frequently cited presenting problems of over fifty thousand youth who received services in two hundred ten runaway shelters in 1984 included: depression, suicidal tendencies, alcohol and drug problems, physical abuse, sexual abuse, and the generic category - severe psychological problems.

The presenting problems of the National Network of Runaway Youth Services (1985) survey corresponds to some of the cluster of behaviors reviewed earlier, i.e. delinquency and psychopathology. Other researchers (Barber & Hosch, 1983; Gilchrist, 1984) have identified some discriminating behaviors associated with runaway behavior. However, the instruments used to identify these behaviors did not seem representative of the range of behaviors associated with the adolescent runaway. In addition, the methodological problems associated with the literature would seem to cast doubt upon the validity of a current psychological profile of an adolescent runaway.

Assessment instrument. The Personality Inventory for Children - Revised is a six hundred true-false item personality inventory used for the assessment of behavior dysfunction in children and adolescents. The informant on the test is the parent, usually the mother, or some other significant adult. The PIC-R contain sixteen profile scales plus four factor scales. Of the sixteen profile scales of the PIC-R, ten scales seemed representative of the range of behaviors associated with adolescent runaways as supported in the literature. Those scales were Adjustment, Intellectual Screening, Development, Anxiety, Withdrawal, Achievement, Depression, Family Relations, Delinquency, and Social Skills.

Lachar (1982) has developed a two hundred eighty item shortened version of the PIC-R. The application of the short form of the Personality Inventory for Children-Revised is useful for two reasons. One, Lachar's (1982) shortened version of the inventory may be completed in approximately thirty to forty five minutes. The brevity is important because runaway shelters are crisis facilities. Crisis facilities emphasize deescalation, stabilization, and homeostasis in working with the adolescent and his or her family. The cooperation of a parent, to take a test, in the midst of a crisis, is inversely related to the brevity of the test. Second, the PIC-R profile scales reflect the presenting problems and other personality characteristics of runaway adolescents as revealed in the literature. A brief description of the scales and their reliability and validity is outlined in Appendix A.

PURPOSE

Due to the lack of an assessment instrument that was representative of the range of behaviors associated with adolescent runaways, the following study was proposed. The purpose of this study was to use a personality measure that was hypothesized as representative of a cluster of behaviors associated with running away and to determine if a predictive equation could be generated by comparing a group of adolescent runaways to two other criterion groups: a psychiatric (henceforth referred to as maladjusted) sample and a control sample, whose subjects had not run away nor had ever been referred to a mental health professional for psychological problems.

RESEARCH QUESTIONS

From the purpose statement, a general research question was derived. Did adolescent runaways exhibit a personality profile which was distinct from other adolescents? From the general research question the following specific research questions were derived.

1. Could male runaways be discriminated from a male control sample and a male maladjusted sample on a personality inventory?

2. Could female runaways be discriminated from a female control sample and a female maladjusted sample on a personality inventory?

From the specific research questions the following hypotheses were proposed.

HYPOTHESES

From research questions one and two the following hypothesis is proposed.

Ho1: There is no difference between males and females, on selected personality scales of the Personality Inventory for Children - Revised (Adjustment, Achievement, Depression, Family Relations, Delinquency, Social Skills), within an adolescent runaway group, an adolescent maladjusted group, and an adolescent control group.

Ho2: There is no difference on selected personality scales of the Personality Inventory for Children - Revised (Adjustment, Achievement, Depression, Family Relations, Delinquency, Social Skills) within an adolescent runaway group, an adolescent maladjusted group, and an adolescent control group.

Ho3: The Personality Inventory for Children - Revised variables (Adjustment, Achievement, Depression, Family Relations, Delinquency, Social Skills) will not predict membership in one of three groups, a control sample, a runaway sample, and a maladjusted sample.

DEFINITION OF TERMS

Adolescent runaway - An adolescent aged 13 through 17 who had run away from home and voluntarily went to the Family Link/Runaway House and was residing there.

Maladjusted sample - A psychiatric criterion group in which all subjects had received a formal Diagnostic and Statistical Manual - III diagnosis indicative of psychological dysfunction.

Control sample - A criterion group in which the adolescent subjects were free from any psychiatric history and had not run away from home.

Personality Inventory for Children - Revised - A 280 item short-form version of a parent informant, 600 true-false item personality inventory containing 16 profile scales which can be subsumed under 4 factor scales. The 16 profile scales are Lie, Frequency, Defensiveness, Adjustment, Intellectual Screening, Developmental, Somatic, Depression, Family Relations, Delinquency, Withdrawal, Anxiety, Psychosis, Hyperactivity, and Social Skills.

ASSUMPTIONS

This study assumes the following:

1) The subjects in the control group had never run away from home and had never seen a mental health professional for an emotional problem.

2) That religious affiliation is not a confounding variable and if ruled out as a confounding variable, the subjects used for the control sample would be appropriate.

3) That there is a cluster of behaviors associated with running away and these behaviors can be identified.

LIMITATIONS

This study is subject to the following limitations:

1) The use of religious affiliated youth in Memphis and Shelby County, Tennessee, for a control group is not a representative sample of youth in Memphis and Shelby County, Tennessee, nor of the United States of America. Therefore, without a stratified random sample, generalization may be compromised.

2) The use of only youth appearing at the Family Link in Memphis, Tennessee, is not representative of all adolescent runaway youth in the United States of America. Different geographical regions may have different rates of presenting problems for runaways. This limits generalization of the findings to other adolescent runaway youth in the United States of America.

3) Just those parents who were willing to fill out the PIC-R may reflect a bias as to whether those youth were similar to those whose parents did not meet the inclusion criteria of willingness to participate in taking the PIC-R.

II

Review of Related Literature

This chapter will focus on the research relevant to the power of standardized, norm referenced instruments used to differentiate runaways from non-runaways. Research on the problems associated with adolescent runaway behavior will also be reviewed. In addition, the instruments representative of this research have been reviewed with regard to their reliability and validity in assessing the problem areas associated with adolescent runaway behavior.

PROBLEMS ASSOCIATED WITH ADOLESCENT RUNAWAY BEHAVIOR

The following six problem areas have been associated with adolescent runaway behavior. They are family relationships, parental problems, delinquent behavior, school problems, peer relationships, and symptoms of psychopathology. In this section of chapter 2, each of the problem areas will detail several supporting studies applicable to the problem. Following the supporting studies, there will be one or more particular studies cited. These particular studies will be reviewed with regard to the measuring instrument used. These particular studies also will be examples of the type of research done relative to each problem area associated with adolescent runaway behavior.

Family relationships. Family relationships is a problem area associated with adolescent runaway behavior. The studies supporting this problem area focus on problems associated with the family system instead of the system's individual members. Moriarity (1975) concluded that running away is a family problem. Within their families, runaways experienced less family interaction, less affection, fewer verbal and physical rewards, and were allowed less independence (Linden, 1979). Linden (1979) also concluded that long term family problems contributed to the youth's internal problems which led to a runaway episode.

Additional family problems were that runaways and their parents reported far less empathy and positive regard from each other than did non-runaways and their parents (Spillaine-Grieco, 1984).

The studies by Steinbock (1977) and Maar (1984) are examples of the type of research conducted and the instruments used in assessing the family relationships of adolescent runaways. Steinbock (1977) explored runaway behavior from a family interaction model. Three groups of families were used. Families of runaways (N = 12), families of non-runaway crises (N = 11), and comparison families (N = 16). Each of these groups was composed of thirty four Caucasian adolescents, age twelve to seventeen years, with a sixty percent female and a forty percent male composition. The Family Environment Scale, Family Life Space Diagram, and the Family Life Crisis Questionnaire were used to assess the families. The behaviors that differentiated the runaway group from the crisis family group were that the adolescent runaways were seen as isolated and separated from the family as seen by both themselves and their parents.

Maar (1984) attempted to identify critical factors that differentiated runaway adolescents from non-runaway adolescents. The Index of Family Relations Scale, the Child's Attitude Toward Mother Scale, the Child's Attitude Toward Father Scale, a behavior checklist, and a demographic questionnaire were used to assess the subjects. The subjects in this sample totaled 1296. The characteristics of the runaways that differentiated them from the non-runaways were: step-parent in the family, negative attitudes toward the parents, and a negative attitude toward family life in general.

In summary, the behaviors that identified the adolescent runaway, in relationship to his or her family, were that they were perceived by themselves and their parents as being isolated from their parents, had negative attitudes toward their parents and family life in general, and that they had a step-parent.

Parental problems. Whereas the problem area of family relationships dealt with problems associated with the family system, the problem area of parental problems focuses on behaviors peculiar to the parents of adolescent runaways. Parental behaviors related to adolescent runaways were studied by several researchers. Arulanandam (1980) found that runaways and delinquent subjects described their mothers and fathers as being significantly higher than normal subjects on variables of possessiveness, rejection, control, inconsistent discipline and instilling persistent anxiety. Analysis indicated no significant difference between the runaway and delinquent subjects' mothers and fathers on the above behaviors. Fry (1982) found that paternal correlates of runaway behavior, with adolescent males and females, were father detachment, relative absence of child centeredness, and degree of communicativeness in the father. Sweeny (1976) concluded that parental attitudes toward their children do influence runaway behavior. Those specific attitudes were rejection, discipline, and indulgence.

Adler (1980) and Van-Houten (1977) both developed their own assessment instruments in an attempt to identify runaway-prone adolescent females. The instruments measured behavioral characteristics attributed to the parents of female adolescent runaways by the runaways and measured characteristics of the runaways themselves.

Adler (1980) developed the Runaway Prone Questionnaire, which is a psychodiagnostic instrument for detecting runaway prone adolescent girls. It was developed by interviewing 800 adolescent girls (actual runaway, runaway prone, and non-runaway prone). A profile of a runaway prone girl emerged and was subsequently applied to an additional 673 adolescent girls. The specifics of the demographic data (age, sex, race) were not available from the abstract. Seven scales emerged from the 50-item test. The instrument's 7 scales were: perceived and actual rejection by parents, perceived and actual invasion of privacy, powerlessness, inadequate coping skills, defiance/rebellion, the loner syndrome, and frustration/escape. A heightened sense of rejection correlated with a runaway prone female profile.

Van-Houten (1977) developed the Life Events Inventory, a measure of stress. The inventory was developed by having a criterion group of 195 high school students rate 83 life events for stress. An analysis based upon a semi-interquartile range discrepancy among the adolescents yielded 62 items. These 62 items then constituted the inventory. The inventory and a demographic questionnaire were then administered to a convenience sample of 349 adolescents that were a non-representative national sample. The 93 runaways were from 6 runaway centers and the 251 non-runaways were selected from 3 cooperating high schools. This study found that one of the strongest predictors of running away was parental rejection.

In summary, the generic behavior that has been identified with parental problems has been that the adolescent runaway has felt rejected by his or her parent.

Delinquent behavior. Runaway behavior has often been described as being a delinquent act. Several studies are cited in support of this problematic area associated with adolescent runaways. Edelbrock (1980) found that outpatient mental health center-referred youth who had run away from home had the Child Behavior Checklist categorical profile of a Delinquent. The behaviors associated with this profile included lying, truancy, stealing, and bad friends. Mitchell and Dodder (1980) found that having delinquent peers enhances the likelihood of becoming delinquent and that pre-delinquent behavior can create the stimulus for running away.

Linden (1980) used the Jesness Inventory, which measures delinquent behavior, in runaway and non-runaway adolescent females. The study sampled 36 female runaways and 36 female non-runaways. Analysis indicated that runaway girls were found to be more delinquent, angry, insecure, depressed, withdrawn, and mistrustful than their non-runaway peers.

In summary, delinquent behaviors have been associated with adolescent runaways. Those behaviors include anger, depression, insecurity, withdrawal, and mistrust.

School problems. In addition to delinquent behavior being characteristic of adolescent runaways, school problems have also been associated with adolescent runaways. Several studies are cited below in support of this problematic area. Brennon, Hiuzinga, and Elliott (1978) suggest that poor school experiences precipitate runaway behavior. Doty (1979) investigated the relationship between the availability of community resources and runaway behavior. The results indicated that prevention of runaway behavior should focus on high risk youth whose families had moved often and youth who were frequently absent from school.

Adler (1980) found that increased school absences and declining grade point averages were significantly correlated with a runaway prone female profile.

Adler (1980) and Van-Houten (1977) developed instruments useful in assessing problems associated with the parents of adolescent runaways. These instruments were also useful in detecting school related problems of the adolescent runaway. Van-Houten (1977), as previously reviewed also found that school dropout status was one of the strongest predictors of running away.

In summary, the school problems associated with adolescent runaways who have been assessed included school absences, declining GPA, and school dropout status.

Peer relationships. An additional problem area associated with adolescent runaways is their social or peer relationships. Gilchrist (1984) found that the runaway adolescent had poor social relationships. Poor problem solving skills, with regard to coping with stress and crises, were also associated with runaways (Roberts, 1982a). Vanderloo (1977) researched coping behavior of runaway adolescents. She found that runaways produced a lesser degree of solutions to problems and fewer active efforts toward reaching a solution than did non-runaways on a story completion measure of parental coercive situations.

The Runaway Prone Questionnaire (Adler, 1980) has apparent utility in assessing behavioral characteristics associated with adolescent runaways. Besides assessing the problem areas of parental problems and school problems, it has also been used in assessing the adolescent runaway's peer relationships. Adler also found that deteriorating coping skills were correlated with a female runaway prone profile. In summary, adolescent female runaways have been assessed as having poor coping skills with regard to peer relationship problems.

Symptoms of psychopathology. The National Network of Runaway and Youth Services survey (NNRYS, 1985) indicated that there are presenting problems associated with adolescent runaways that seem symptomatic of psychopathology. Several investigators cite evidence in support of this problem area being associated with adolescent runaways. Scalf (1978) found that runaway youth had a lower self-esteem than did non-runaways. Gutierres and Riech (1981) found that physical and sexual abuse was associated with adolescent runaway behavior. Hughes (1981) also found sexual abuse associated with runaway female adolescents. Harris (1980) found that in a sample of high school dropouts who had experienced traumatic life events, that additional symptomatic behaviors were associated with the trauma. These behaviors were suicide attempts, running away, drug use, and delinquency. Steinbock (1977) found that the behaviors associated with the families of runaways included physical abuse and Maar (1984) found that alcohol and drug usage by the runaway was a characteristic that differentiated families of runaways from non-runaway families.

Phillips (1976) used the Rutgers Self-Descriptive Questionnaire-- Parts I and II to assess depression and dysphoria and the High School Personality Questionnaire to assess general personality traits. In this study of 43 runaway repeater girls and 43 non-runaway girls, a profile of a female runaway repeater was determined. He found that the runaway repeater girls had depression prone personality traits while non-runaway girls did not.

Burke (1985) evaluated the personality and psychological characteristics of runaways and non-runaways. The subjects totaled 199 males, ages 12 - 18, all of whom were residents in a treatment center. The subjects were assessed using the Millon Adolescent Personality Inventory (MAPI). Factor analysis and discriminant analysis did not yield a discriminant function that could effectively classify the two groups. The findings were that the runaways and non-runaways were similar in that they presented as lonely, insecure, had poor impulse control, and had an unwillingness to comply with social regulation. The only differences between the two groups were that, in terms of an unwillingness to comply with social regulation, the runaways were aggressive in their resistance to compliance while the non-runaways behaved in a passive defiant manner. Burke concluded that runaway and non-runaway male adolescents in residential treatment centers were not significantly different from each other and that the differences that were found were very subtle.

In summary, the assessed symptoms of psychopathology that have been associated with adolescent runaways included depression and poor impulse control.

The above review identified six problem areas and corresponding behaviors associated with adolescent runaways. These problem areas were family relationships, parental problems, delinquent behavior, school problems, peer relationships, and symptoms of psychopathology. The corresponding behaviors associated with these problem areas included less family interaction, less empathy, adolescent alcohol and drug use, delinquent behavior, poor school performance, poor coping skills, depression, and poor impulse control.

INSTRUMENTS

The foregoing research, and the assessment instruments used are representative examples of research that focuses on the six problematic areas (family relationships, parental problems, delinquent behavior, school problems, peer relationships, and symptoms of psychopathology) and corresponding behaviors of adolescent runaways. The instruments used in the reviewed research were the Family Environment Scale, Family Life Space Diagram, Family Life Crisis Questionnaire, The Index of Family Relations Scale, Child's Attitude Toward Mother Scale, Child's Attitude Towards Father, The Runaway Prone Questionnaire, Life Events Inventory, Rutgers Self Descriptive Questionnaire - Parts I and II, the High School Personality Questionnaire, the Jesness Inventory, and the Millon Adolescent Personality Inventory.

The foregoing tests were reviewed and used as examples of research on assessing the problems and behaviors associated with adolescent runaways. A further review of the relevance of these tests to the six problematic areas associated with adolescent runaway behavior was done by examining professional reviews and critiques of these tests. Of the twelve tests cited as examples of research relevant to the problematic areas associated with male and female adolescent runaway behavior, professional critiques were found only for the Family Environment Scale, the Jesness Inventory, the Millon Adolescent Personality Inventory and the High School Personality Questionnaire. A summary of the reviews and critiques for these four professionally critiqued tests will be presented with regard to their relevance in the assessment of the problematic areas associated with adolescent runaway behavior.

Family Environment Scale. The Family Environment Scale (FES) was used to assess the problematic area of family relationships. Sweetland and Keyser (1986) as quoted in Tests state that the FES is a:

> 90-item paper and pencil test measuring ten dimensions (scales) of family environments. These dimensions are further grouped into three categories: relationships, personal growth, and system maintenance. (p. 73)

Some of the behaviors associated with this problematic area are that the adolescent has a negative attitude toward his parents and toward family life in general, has a step-parent, and that the runaway feels isolated from the family. The runaways also believe that their families are conflictual, intolerable, have communication problems, have sibling rivalry problems, a separation, divorce, or death in the family, and feelings of rejection by parents. The following reviews describe the validity and reliability of the Family Environment Scale.

Dreyer (1978) in his review of the FES in The Eighth Mental Measurements Yearbook, indicated that the authors assume that family environments have "personalities" which, like individual personalities, can be measured. Dreyer (1978) reported that:

> Subscale correlations for internal consistency range from .45 to .58. The test-retest reliability correlations over an eight week interval vary from .68 to .86 depending on the scale ... their discussion of the validity is disappointing. (p. 821)

The authors of the FES provide no validity studies on their instrument except for face validity. Sines (1978) states that " . . . there is no empirical evidence that the FES taps the important features of family environments" (p. 822).

In a later review, Bush-Rossangel (1985) commented: "no information is provided about the rationale for selecting the ten subscales which were included or the three underlying domains" (p. 408).

Concerning the norms for the FES, there are only norms for the control family, even though the item selection process included a national cross-section of "distressed" families. In conclusion, "The FES should not be used at this time for clinical or decision making purposes" (Sines, 1978, p. 822).

The Jesness Inventory. The Jesness Inventory (JI) has been used to assess the problematic area of delinquency. Sweetland and Keyser (1986) as quoted in Tests, stated that the purpose of the JI is to:

> Evaluate personality disorders predictive of a-social tendencies. Used to classify disturbed children and adolescents for treatment. Distinguishes delinquents from non-delinquents. (Sweetland & Keyser, 1986, p. 159)

Some of the behaviors associated with this problematic area are: lying, stealing, having bad friends, and having delinquent peers. Other behaviors associated with this problem area are being defiant, disobeying rules, being truant from school, and using alcohol and drugs. The following reviews describe the validity and reliability of the JI.

The JI is a 155-item test consisting of 11 personality characteristics or constructs. Scores from the inventory are used in the classification of juvenile offenders into a theoretical typology of integration levels and subtypes. The reliability and validity studies of the JI are suspect. The author claims a 84 percent accuracy in separating male or female delinquents from non-delinquents but there is no reliability data for females or for one of the primary scales, the Asocial Index. Split-half reliabilities range from .62 to .88 for the subscales and stability estimates range from .40 to .70.

Butt (1978) comments in her review of the JI that there is a weakness in the selection of the constructs or scales. The author defines the scales theoretically but provides no validational support for them. There is considerable overlap in the scales and the original source for the scale items is usually not specified. The norms that are reported are 1961 and 1962 data. Butt agreed with the author of the JI that the test is best used as a screening device and also advised its use for experimental and research work. Butt (1978) concluded that:

> It appears that the inventory is best suited for experimental and exploratory work, such as in research, or as a basis for possible discussion with individual delinquents, or as a rough initial screening instrument. (p. 595)

Millon Adolescent Personality Inventory. The Millon Adolescent Personality Inventory (MAPI) is used to assess the symptoms of psychopathology. Sweetland and Keyser (1986) as quoted in Tests, state that the MAPI is used to: evaluate adolescent personality as an aid to clinical assessment and identifies student behavioral and emotional problems (p. 118). Some of the behaviors associated with symptomatic pathological problems are low self-esteem, physical abuse, and sexual abuse. Additional behaviors are stealing, disobedience, truancy, depression, suicidal tendencies, alcohol and drug problems, and the generic category of severe psychological problems. The following reviews describe the validity and reliability of the MAPI.

Brown (1985) comments that the MAPI is a 150-item, 20 scale test that has three dimensions. The intent of the instrument is to provide a diagnostic and classification system for adolescent behaviors as well as providing personality descriptions. Reliability is based on test-retest and internal consistency data. The reliability coefficients range from .45 to .84 for the subscales. There is concurrent validity with the California Psychological Inventory and the 16PF but no comparison was done with the adolescent norms of the MMPI. Brown also points out that the factor analytic data does not particularly support the underlying structure of the instrument.

Widiger (1985) in his review concludes that there is a " ... paucity of empirical support for 16 of the 20 MAPI scales" (p. 980). No cross-validation studies were conducted for predictive accuracy and " ... because validity data are essentially lacking, publication at this time is premature" (p. 980).

High School Personality Questionnaire. The High School Personality Questionnaire (HSPQ) was also used to assess the problematic area of symptoms of psychopathology. The HSPQ was cited in Tests (Sweetland & Keyser, 1986). Its citation states that it:

> Identifies adolescents with high potentials for dropping out of school, drug abuse, and low achievement. Used in correctional situations to facilitate parent-teacher, parent-officer, and parent-clinic cooperation. (Sweetland & Keyser, 1986, p. 140)

The behaviors associated with this problematic area were outlined under the previously mentioned test, the MAPI. The following reviews describe the validity and reliability of the HSPQ.

> Hogan (1972), in his review of the HSPQ, states that the: HSPQ was designed to measure 12 of the 16 factors appearing on Cattell's (author) Sixteen Personality Factor Questionnaire. [However] there does not appear to be a consistent comparability between the scales common to the HSPQ and the 16PF. The correlations range from .03 to .71. (Buros, 1972, p. 207)

Hogan further points out in his review that concurrent validity is lacking in that no information is provided about the HSPQ and its relation to external criteria or other personality and interest measures. Hogan (1972) concludes that the HSPQ " ... seems to represent only overt self-description; the reliability of the scales is modest and their validity is indeterminate."

Jackson (1972) reviewed the HSPQ and concluded that:

> The nature of its subject matter (personality), the technical inadequacies and omissions in the handbook, and the relative sophistication required properly to evaluate the author's unsupported and often unsupportable assertions regarding the test suggest that it should be used if at all only by test specialists and only for research purposes. (Buros, 1972, p. 209)

Conclusions. The Mental Measurements Yearbook and Tests are compendiums of reviews and critiques of tests and inventories that are used by the professional community. The four tests that were reviewed, the Family Environment Scale, the Jesness Inventory, the Millon Adolescent Personality Inventory, and the High School Personality Questionnaire are tests used by mental health professionals. These four tests were reviewed and critiqued as being examples of instruments used in assessing the problems associated with adolescent runaways. The conclusions of the reviewers of the tests are summarized below with regard to the tests' validity and reliability for the assessment of the problems associated with adolescent runaways as reviewed in the literature.

1. The reliability of the Family Environment Scale was relatively sound but no validity studies were provided.

2. The Jesness Inventory has reliability data for males but none for females. There is no validational data provided for the scales of the Jesness Inventory.

3. The reliability of the Millon Personality Inventory is relatively acceptable, but there is very little empirical support for 16 of the 20 subscales. Validational data is lacking.

4. The reliability of the High School Personality Questionnaire is modest and validational data is lacking.

The reliability and validity of the Family Environment Scale, the Jesness Inventory, the Millon Adolescent Personality Inventory, and the High School Personality Questionnaire were summarized from the reviews and critiques found in the professional literature. It may be concluded from the reviews that these instruments, which were representative of the instruments used in the assessment of problems associated with adolescent runaways, are inadequate choices in assessing the problems of adolescent runaways. The reliability of the reviewed instruments seemed barely acceptable and the validity of the instruments was non-existent. In other words, it is not known what is being measured and the conjectured traits are being measured in an inconsistent manner. What seems to be needed is: first, evidence of an assessment instrument that is representative of the range of behavior problems runaway adolescents experience and, second, whether this instrument might accurately determine a cluster of behaviors or profile associated with adolescent runaway behavior and, finally, based upon this profile, could runaways be discriminated from non-runaway criterion groups.

Summary. This chapter reviewed research on behaviors associated with the problems experienced by adolescent runaways. In addition, examples of research, with the corresponding instruments used for assessing those problems, were presented. The appropriateness of the instruments used in assessing the problems was reviewed for professional use.

The validity and reliability, and therefore the appropriateness, of the instruments in use presently is questioned. The instruments used did assess some of the behaviors associated with adolescent runaways, as reviewed in the literature, but those instruments had barely acceptable reliability and no validity relative to the problems experienced by adolescent runaways.

Finally, with regard to the reviews and critiques, it was concluded that the reviewed instruments were not appropriate for the assessment of the problematic areas associated with adolescent runaway behavior.

III

Methodology

SAMPLE AND POPULATION

Runaway sample. The target group was all of the runaway residents who resided at the Memphis, TN Family Link/Runaway House between 1986 through 1988, and whose custodian (primarily female) completed the Personality Inventory for Children - Revised. There were 63 protocols but two were eliminated due to being invalid resulting in a sample of 61.

Control sample. This group consisted of 60 adolescent subjects, male and female, aged 13 through 17. These subjects were members of various church youth groups and had never run away from home nor had seen a mental health professional.

Maladjusted sample. Dr. David Lachar, one of the developers of the PIC-R, was contacted and asked to cooperate in this study by supplying a stratified random sample of 59 PIC-R protocols of maladjusted adolescents aged 13 through 17. These 59 protocols were from a larger sample of 1226 subjects seen at an outpatient clinic in Detroit, Michigan, for problematic behavioral and emotional adjustment. The subjects in this maladjusted sample had DSM-III diagnoses of depression, mental retardation, learning disability, hyperactivity, anxiety, psychotic, and adjustment reaction of adolescence.

For the purposes of this study those subjects from the maladjusted sample who had the diagnosis of conduct disorder were excluded from this sample. The reason for exclusion was that one of the criteria for the diagnosis of conduct disorder was running away. To eliminate this possible confounding variable the conduct disordered subjects were not used in the maladjusted group.

INSTRUMENTATION

The Personality Inventory for Children - Revised (Lachar, 1984) was originally a 600 true-false item personality inventory that contained 16 profile scales plus four factor scales. With Lachar's (1982) shortened version of 280 items, the clinical appeal of the Personality Inventory for Children - Revised increased. Estimates of internal consistency were computed for both the original and shortened forms. There was no significant change in internal consistency associated with the scale item reduction. Test-retest reliability indicated that the shortened version retained the temporal stability of its full-length counterpart.

Correlations between the shortened and full-length versions of the PIC-R were from .88 to .89 (Forbes, 1986). The percentage of clinical interpretive agreement between the original and shortened version scales was from 92% to 97% (Lachar, 1982).

Selected scales - Adjustment, Intellectual Screening, Developmental, Anxiety, Withdrawal, Achievement, Depression, Family Relations, Delinquency, and Social Skills - were representative of a cluster of behaviors associated with adolescent runaway behavior as revealed in the literature on this topic. These variables were used to determine if, as a set, they could differentiate between three criterion groups; a runaway sample, an adolescent normal sample, and an adolescent maladjusted sample.

DATA COLLECTION

Runaway sample. The custodians who attended at least one family therapy session and who had adolescents residing at the Family Link/Runaway House between 1986 and 1988 were asked to complete the Personality Inventory for Children - Revised during the first therapy session. The inventories that met the criteria of being completed and valid were eligible for inclusion in this sample. The total sample size was 61 with there being 11 males (18%) and 50 females (82%). Sixty-three percent were white and 37% were black. The age range was from 13 through 17. No 18-year-olds were included.

Control sample. Youth ministers of various cooperating churches and synagogues in Memphis, Tennessee, were contacted in the fall of 1989 and asked to distribute introductory letters explaining the purpose of this study to their adolescent members. Permission forms were also distributed. Those parents signing and returning the permission forms were mailed the PIC-R, and were asked to complete and return the inventory. Those protocols that met the criteria of inclusion and were valid were used in this sample. The total sample size was 60. Males comprised 43% of the sample and females 56%. Ninety-three percent of the sample was white and 7% was black.

Maladjusted sample. These 59 protocols were from a larger sample of 1226 subjects seen at an outpatient clinic in Detroit, Michigan in 1979, for problematic behavioral and emotional adjustment. This sample was comprised of males (50%) and females (50%). Fifty percent were white and fifty percent were black.

STATISTICAL ANALYSIS

Design. Since this was a study limited to naturally occurring rather than experimentally manipulated variables, the research design chosen was an ex post facto design. This design was chosen because the runaway sample consisted of the 61 subjects whose parent completed a valid PIC-R during the years 1986 to 1988.

Selected scales. Examination of the selected scales Adjustment, Intellectual Screening, Development, Anxiety, Withdrawal, Achievement, Depression, Family Relations, Delinquency, and Social Skills indicated that some were redundant. These scales were selected because they seem reflective of the characteristics associated with adolescent runaways as reviewed in the literature. According to the manual for the PIC-R (Lachar, 1984), Achievement correlated with the Development and Intellectual Screening scales .84 and .56 respectively. Intellectual Screening correlated with Development .74. Therefore, it was decided that the Intellectual Screening and Development scales not be included in the representative cluster of behaviors associated with adolescent runaway behavior.

The Withdrawal and Anxiety scales were also excluded. The Depression scale correlated with the Withdrawal and Anxiety scales .62 and .81 respectively.

While Depression also correlated with Social Skills .62 it was decided to include Social Skills because this scale correlated significantly with the Schizophrenia scale of the Minnesota Multiphasic Personality Inventory (Pipp, 1979). The relationship between a PIC-R scale and a known measure of psychopathology is made as an attempt to operationally define 'severe psychological problems' which is one of the main presenting problems of adolescent runaways (NNRYS, 1985). The Social Skills scale was the PIC-R scale that most represented this behavior of adolescent runaways as revealed in the literature.

Demographic variables. The demographic variables race and sex were to be included in the representative cluster of associated characteristics of adolescent runaways. However, in the development of the norms for the analysis of the PIC, data indicated that separate norms for sex was necessary (Wirt et al., 1984). Later research indicated that the effects of race and sex:

> do not systematically bias the obtained PIC scale elevations and the results do not present either a consistent or a pervasive relationship between PIC scale elevations and race or sex. (Wirt, et al., 1984, p. 115)

This apparent inconsistency is due to the conversion of raw scores to T scores. This conversion to T scores normalized the gender differences. Therefore, subsequent research after the norming of the PIC did not reflect gender differences. Since separate norms for sex had already been constructed for the PIC and since race demonstrated no consistent effect, the variables sex and race were excluded from the representative cluster of associated characteristics of adolescent runaway behavior.

STATISTICAL PROCEDURES

The selected statistics used in the proposed study were as follows.

Homogeneity of control sample. A one-way analysis of variance (ANOVA) was used to determine if the mean PIC-R scores of the control subjects from the different religious affiliations (i.e., Baptist, Presbyterian, Catholic, Episcopalian, Jewish, Methodist, and unclassified) were significantly different.

Extension of age norms. Since the PIC-R age norms are 3 through 16½, could seventeen-year-olds be included in this group also? Developmentally, there seems to be no reason why the age range of the norms of the PIC-R could not be extended to include seventeen-year-olds (Lachar & Gdowski, 1979; Lachar, Gdowski, & Snyder, 1984). On the selected scales, maturational events in this age group should have no significant effect on the dependent variables. Therefore, a two-way analysis of variance was used to test to see if seventeen-year-olds differed significantly from thirteen- through sixteen-year-olds.

Outliers. Since multivariant outliers can bias the results, Mahalanobis Distance (factor analysis) was used to determine if there were outliers (Klecka, 1980).

Gender differences. To determine if there were gender differences within the three groups and if merging the sexes within each group was statistically possible, a multivariate analysis of variance (MANOVA) was conducted.

Group differences. To determine if the three groups significantly differed from each other, a one-way analysis of variance and Scheffé's test for post-hoc analysis was conducted.

Group classification. Discriminant analysis was used to determine the significance between the groups, to establish a predictive equation, and to classify subjects on the significant predictive variables.

Split-sample validation. To determine the efficacy of the derived discriminate functions, a cross-validation procedure was conducted (Klecka, 1980).

The results of the analyses are reported in the following chapter.

IV

Results

RELIGIOUS GROUPS

The first antecedent test for testing the hypotheses was to determine if there were significant differences between religious affiliation subgroups within the control group. It was thought the possibility existed that religious affiliation would influence the personality profile of the subjects. Thus, the control group would not be homogeneous. A frequency distribution of the religious affiliated subgroups is listed in Table 1.

TABLE 1
FREQUENCY DISTRIBUTION OF RELIGIOUS AFFILIATED SUBGROUPS

Group	Frequency	Percent
Jewish	21	35.0
Methodist	1	1.0
Episcopalian	7	11.0
Baptist	18	30.0
Catholic	2	3.0
Unclassified	10	16.0
Presbyterian	1	1.0
Total	60	100.0

Because the 'n' of the Methodist, Catholic, and Presbyterian cells were small, for statistical purposes, these three groups were combined.

Combining these cells resulted in there being five religious affiliated subgroups (see Table 2).

TABLE 2

FREQUENCY DISTRIBUTION OF COMBINED
RELIGIOUS AFFILIATED SUBGROUPS

Group	Frequency	Percent
Jewish	21	35.0
Episcopalians	7	11.7
Baptist	18	30.0
Unclassified	10	16.7
Methodist/Catholic		
Presbyterian	4	6.7
Total	60	100.0

A one-way analysis of variance was performed to see if there were mean differences between the religious groups on the Personality Inventory for Children - Revised scales of Adjustment, Achievement, Depression, Family Relations, Delinquency, and Social Skills. A summary of the F ratios for the ANOVA for the religious groups is provided in Table 3. The religious subgroups were not significantly different from each other on the following PIC-R Scales: Adjustment $F(4, 55) = 1.13$, $p > .05$; Achievement $F(4, 55) = .67$, $p > .05$; Family Relations $F(4, 55) = .17$, $p > .05$; Delinquency $F(4, 55) = .83$, $p > .05$; Social Skills $F(4, 55) = .36$, $p > .05$.

On the Depression scale, the Baptist subgroup was significantly different from the combined Methodist/Catholic/Presbyterian subgroup $F(4, 55) = 2.41$, $p < .05$. While a statistically significant difference ($p < .05$) exists between these two groups, the difference did not reach a clinical interpretive cutoff score on the PIC-R. Therefore the combined Methodist/Catholic/Presbyterian group could not be perceived as depressed. The ANOVA tables for religious affiliation are presented in Appendix C.

The analysis of whether religious affiliation would influence scale elevation on the PIC-R indicated that religious affiliation did not influence PIC-R scale elevation. The mean scores for the religious groups on each variable closely approximated the mean for the standardization of the PIC which was a T score of 50. This analysis supports the use of adolescent youth from religious affiliated groups as research control subjects.

TABLE 3
SUMMARY OF F-RATIOS FOR RELIGIOUS SUBGROUPS

Scale					F-Ratio
Adjustment	F	(4,55)	=	1.13,	p>.05
Achievement	F	(4,55)	=	.67,	p>.05
Depression	F	(4,55)	=	2.41,	p<.05 *
Family Relations	F	(4,55)	=	.17,	p>.05
Delinquency	F	(4,55)	=	.83,	p>.05
Social Skills	F	(4,55)	=	.36,	p>.05

AGE NORMS

An antecedent test to determine homogeneity was performed to determine if the age norms (3-16 1/2) for the PIC-R could be extended upward to include seventeen-year-olds. Including the seventeen-year-olds in all the groups would give the groups equal n. If the cell or group sizes are equal, the ANOVA is not as sensitive to the violations of homogeneity of variance (Shavelson, 1981). A frequency distribution of ages for the subjects across the three groups is listed in Table 4.

TABLE 4

FREQUENCY DISTRIBUTION OF SUBJECTS' AGES
ACROSS ALL GROUPS

Group	Frequency	Percent
13 year-olds	28	15.5
14 year-olds	39	21.7
15 year-olds	55	30.6
16 year-olds	38	21.1
17 year-olds	20	11.1
Total	180	100.0

A two-way analysis of variance was performed in which the dependent variables were the PIC-R scales of Adjustment, Achievement, Depression, Family Relations, Delinquency, and Social Skills. A main effect was the Criterion Group (control - 1, runaway -2, and maladjusted - 3) The other main effect was Age Group (13-16 year-olds and 17-year-olds). In all calculations there were no two-way interactions between 13-16 year-olds and 17-year-olds and no main effect differences due to age groups at the alpha level of .05 (see Appendix D, Tables 1 - 6). A summary of the F ratios for the two-way ANOVA for age groups by PIC-R Scales is provided in Table 5. These results indicate that the PIC-R norms could be extended to include 17-year-olds for the purposes of the study.

OUTLIERS

The next antecedent test was to determine if there were any outliers in the total sample. Outliers or "deviant points" can drastically change the pattern of the relationship between variables. Mahalanobis Distance was used to determine outliers. Mahalanobis Distance is a Chi-square value used to determine the distance between each case score and the group centroid. Scores that are extreme and contribute to making the score pattern unusual are deleted. Eleven cases were identified and deleted leaving a total of 169 cases over three groups.

By deleting the outliers the assumption of homogeneity of variance is attempted to be met. An additional step that was taken to not violate this assumption was to have the groups of equal n. In the use of discriminate analysis a good indicator of whether this assumption is violated is the classification rate. If high and there were violations, they would be minor in which case discriminate analysis would not be sensitive to this degree of violation.

TABLE 5
SUMMARY OF F-RATIOS FOR AGE GROUPS

SCALE				F-RATIO	
ADJ	Main Effect p>.05	F	$(1,174) =$	1.18,	
	2-Way Interaction	F	$(2,174) =$	.93,	p>.05
ACH	Main Effect	F	$(1,174) =$	2.13,	p>.05
	2-Way Interaction	F	$(2,174) =$	.20,	p>.05
DEP	Main Effect	F	$(1,174) =$	.56,	p>.05
	2-Way Interaction	F	$(2,174) =$	.18,	p>.05
FAM	Main Effect	F	$(1,174) =$	.28,	p>.05
	2-Way Interaction	F	$(2,174) =$	.02,	p>.05
DLQ	Main Effect	F	$(1,174) =$	.09,	p>.05
	2-Way Interaction	F	$(2,174) =$	.63,	p>.05
SSK	Main Effect	F	$(1,174) =$	.00,	p>.05
	2-Way Interaction	F	$(2,174) =$	.22,	p>.05

HYPOTHESIS 1

Ho1: There is no difference between males and females, on selected personality scales of the Personality Inventory for Children - Revised (Adjustment, Achievement, Depression, Family Relations, Delinquency, Social Skills), within a sample of adolescent runaways, a maladjusted adolescent sample, and a control sample.

A multivariate analysis of variance (MANOVA) was used to determine if there were significant differences within each group due to gender. Wilks Lambda was $F(12, 316) = .992$, $p > .05$ (see Appendix E, Table 1). These results indicated that within each of the three criterion groups (control, runaway, and maladjusted) on each scale there was not a significant difference ($p > .05$) between the male and female subjects.

While there was not a significant difference ($p > .05$) between the male and female subjects within each of the three groups, there was a significant difference (p < .05) between the sexes across the three groups. The inclusion of the control group probably contributed to the gender effect between groups because of its lower mean.

Due to there being no significant differences (p < .05) between male and female subjects within each of the three criterion groups, the male and female subjects in each group were merged. The null hypothesis was therefore rejected.

HYPOTHESIS 2

Ho2: There is no difference on selected personality scales of the Personality Inventory for Children - Revised (Adjustment, Achievement, Depression, Family Relations, Delinquency, and Social Skills) among a sample of adolescent runaways, a maladjusted adolescent sample and a control sample.

A one-way analysis of variance (see Appendix F) was calculated across the six PIC-R variables to determine if there were significant differences (p < .05) between the three groups (see Appendix F, Tables 1 - 12). Where significance was found, Scheffe's test for post-hoc analysis was calculated to determine which specific groups were significantly different from each other.

Adjustment. For the Adjustment scale there was a significant difference between the samples with F(2, 166) = 158.88, p < .05 (see Appendix F, Table 1). The critical value of Scheffe's test was 9.29 and based on that value the following significant differences were found. The control sample mean score (M = 49.62) was significantly different (p < .05) from the runaway sample mean score (M = 88.80) and the maladjusted sample mean score (M = 85.77). The runaway sample was not significantly different (p > .05) from the maladjusted sample (see Appendix F, Table 2).

Achievement. For the Achievement scale there was a significant difference between the samples with F(2, 166) = 41.46, p < .05 (see Appendix F, Table 3). The critical value of Scheffe's test was 7.99 and based on that value the following significant differences were found. The control sample mean score (M = 45.23) was significantly different (p < .05) from the runaway sample mean score (M = 60.64) and the maladjusted sample mean score (M = 62.92). The runaway sample was not significantly different (p > .05) from the maladjusted sample (see Appendix F, Table 4).

Depression. For the Depression scale there was a significant difference between the samples with F(2, 166) = 52.22, p < .05 (see Appendix F, Table 5). The critical value of Scheffe's test was 8.66 and based on that value the following significant differences were found. The control sample mean score (M = 51.54) was significantly different (p < .05) from the runaway sample mean score (M = 71.42) and the maladjusted sample mean score (M = 72.11). The runaway sample and the maladjusted samples were not significantly different (p > .05) from each other (see Appendix F, Table 6).

Family relations. For the Family Relations scale there was a significant difference between the samples F(2, 166) = 42.15, p < .05 (see Appendix F, Table 7). The Scheffe's test critical value was 6.64 and based on that value, the following significant differences were found. The control sample mean score (M = 48.50) was significantly different (p < .05) from the runaway sample mean score (M = 61.05) and the maladjusted sample mean score (M = 63.56). The runaway sample was not significantly different (p > .05) from the maladjusted sample (see Appendix F, Table 8).

Delinquency. For the Delinquency scale there was a significant difference between the samples F(2, 166) = 197.36, p < .05 (see Appendix F, Table 9). The Scheffe's test critical value was 10.76 and based on that value the following significant differences were found. The control sample mean score (M = 50.00) was significantly different (p < .05) from the runaway sample mean score (M = 102.73) and the maladjusted sample mean score (M = 93.13). There was also a significant difference (p < .05) between the runaway sample (M = 102.73) and maladjusted sample (M = 93.13) (see Appendix F, Table 10).

Social skills. For the Social Skills scale there was a significant difference between the samples F(2, 166) = 67.83, p < .05 (see Appendix F, Table 11). The critical value of Scheffe's test was 8.66 and based on that value the following differences were found. The control sample mean score (M = 43.27) was significantly different (p < .05) from the runaway sample mean score (M = 65.15) and the maladjusted sample mean score (M = 67.35). The runaway sample was not significantly different (p > .05) from the maladjusted sample (see Appendix F, Table 12).

The above calculations indicate that the runaway and maladjusted samples could be significantly (p < .05) distinguished from the control sample on all 6 of the PIC-R variables. The null hypothesis was therefore rejected.

The results of the evaluation of hypothesis two predicted that there was a significant difference (p < .05) between the control sample and the runaway and maladjusted samples on all of the 6 PIC-R variables. The results also indicated that the runaway sample and maladjusted sample were not significantly different (p > .05) from each other on the PIC-R variables except for Delinquency. With the Delinquency variable, while both the runaway and maladjusted samples were significantly different (p < .05) from the control sample, the runaway sample had a higher mean score than the maladjusted sample.

Given these results, it would seem expeditious to combine the runaway and maladjusted samples and calculate a step-wise discriminate analysis to predict membership into one of two groups, a control sample or a runaway/maladjusted sample.

HYPOTHESIS 3

Ho3: The Personality Inventory for Children - Revised variables (Adjustment, Achievement, Depression, Family Relations, Delinquency, Social Skills) will not predict membership in one of two groups, a control sample or a runaway/maladjusted sample.

A step-wise discriminate analysis was conducted. In Table 6, the intercorrelation coefficients of the PIC-R subscales are shown.

TABLE 6
POOLED WITHIN-GROUPS CORRELATION MATRIX OF DISCRIMINATING VARIABLES

	ADJ	ACH	DEP	FAM	DLQ	SSK
ADJ	1.000					
ACH	0.479	1.000				
DEP	0.586	0.342	1.000			
FAM	0.057	0.081	0.233	1.000		
DLQ	0.540	0.146	0.213	0.037	1.000	
SSK	0.579	0.382	0.593	-0.024	0.184	1.000

The highest correlation was the Depression scale which correlated .59 with the Social Skills scale. Next was Adjustment which correlated with Depression = .58, Social Skills = .57, and Delinquency =

.54. However, the intercorrelational matrix did not indicate any significant redundant variables.

DISCRIMINATE FUNCTION

Table 7 indicates the similarity between the variables and the discriminate function. The variables (scales)

Adjustment and Delinquency had correlations of .82 and .80, respectively. As such, these variables will have greater impact on classification rates and enhance the functions' predictive power. Next the standardized canonical discriminate coefficients are discussed.

Table 8 displays the standardized canonical discriminate coefficients with Delinquency and Adjustment being the most important determinants in the function followed by Family Relations, Social Skills, and Depression. The Achievement variable did not add specificity to the predictive power of the canonical function and was dropped. The total canonical correlation was .86 and the Chi-square was significant (X", 5 = 167.75, p < .001). These findings indicate that a relatively strong relationship exists between the groups and variables.

TABLE 7
POOLED WITHIN GROUPS CORRELATIONS BETWEEN DISCRIMINANT VARIABLES AND CANONICAL DISCRIMINANT FUNCTION

Variable	Correlation
Adjustment	.821
Delinquency	.806
Social Skills	.510
Depression	.428
Achievement	.369
Family Relations	.357

Table 9 shows the relative strength and direction of each variable by its unstandardized canonical discriminate coefficient. These coefficients form the functional equation for predicting membership in the groups. Each coefficient, when multiplied by the corresponding PIC-R T-score and added together plus the constant, will yield a sum. This sum is then compared to the cut-off score, which is determined by adding the group means or centroids and dividing by two. The cut-off score is -0.63794. If the functional equation score is higher than the cut-off score, then the subject is classified into group two (runaway/maladjusted sample); if it is lower, then the classification is into group one (control sample).

TABLE 8
STANDARDIZED CANONICAL DISCRIMINANT
FUNCTION COEFFICIENTS - FUNCTION 1

Variable Coefficient	Canonical Correlation	Chi- Square	Significance
DLQ 0.526			
ADJ 0.486			
FAM 0.366			
SSK 0.268			
DEP -0.215	.86	167.754	.0000

* p<.001

TABLE 9
UNSTANDARDIZED CANONICAL DISCRIMINANT
FUNCTION COEFFICIENTS

Variable	Function One
Adjustment	.03896730
Family Relations	.03767356
Delinquency	.03233445
Social Skills	.02206065
Depression	-.01714868
(Constant)	-7.919561

The total accuracy of prediction was 96.83 percent with 100 percent (41) of the control group being correctly placed and 95.3 percent (81) of the runaway/maladjusted group being correctly placed with only 4.7 percent (4) incorrectly placed.

CLASSIFICATION

The classification results are presented in Table 10.

TABLE 10
CLASSIFICATION RESULTS FOR CASES SELECTED
FOR USE IN THE DISCRIMINANT ANALYSIS

Actual Group	No. of Membership Cases Group 2	Predicted Group 1	
Group 1	41	41	0
Control		100.00%	0.0%
Control 2	85	4	81
Runaway		4.7%	95.3%

Percent of "Grouped" Cases Correctly Classified: 96.83%

In discriminate analysis, if the functional equation is applied to the same group from which it is derived, the percent of correct classification becomes inflated. To control for this inflation, the functional equation was applied to a cross-validation group. Table 11 shows that

TABLE 11
CLASSIFICATION RESULTS FOR CROSS-VALIDATION SAMPLE

Actual Group	No. Of Cases	Predicted Group 1	Membership Group 2
Group 1 Control	18	17 94.4%	1 5.6%
Group 2 Runaway	25	2 8.0%	23 92.0%

Percent of "Grouped" Cases Correctly Classified: 93.02% the total accuracy of prediction was 93.02 percent with 94.4 percent (17) of the control group being correctly placed and 5.6 percent (1) incorrectly placed. With the runaway/maladjusted group 92.0 percent (23) were correctly placed, and only 8.0 percent (2) were incorrectly placed.

The group centroids were -2.46479 for group 1 (control), and 1.18890 for group 2 (runaway/maladjusted). The profile is distinctly bimodal and reflects the high percentage of correct classifications by the discriminate function.

The results of the discriminant analysis indicated that five personality scales, Adjustment, Family Relations, Delinquency, Social Skills, and Depression, did predict criterion group membership. On the selected variables, the relationship between the groups and the discriminate function was .86. The split-sample procedure produced a first group correct classification percentage of 96.83%. The second group, for cross-validation purposes, had a 93.03% correct classification rate. The third hypothesis was therefore rejected.

A histogram showing the classification of cases into control and runaway/maladjusted groups is shown in Figure 1.

FIGURE 1

CANONICAL DISCRIMINANT FUNCTION 1

```
16+
    \
     \
      \
12+
      \
       \
        \        1              2      2
         \       1              2      22
 8+       \      1              2      22
           \     1              22 2   22
            \  1 111         2   2222  222
             \ 111111       22   2222 22222
 4+           \ 11111111  2 2  222  2222222222  2
               \ 111111111 211  222222222222222  22
                \ 111111111 211  222222222222222  222
                 \ 1111111112111221222222222222222222

        X----+----+----+----+----+----+----+----+
        x    -3   -2   -1    0   +1   +2   +3   +4
                   1 = Control      2 = R/M
                   M = -2.46        M = 1.18
```

V

Summary, Conclusions, and Recommendations

SUMMARY

Nature and scope. The study investigated the use of a personality measure that was hypothesized to be representative of a cluster of behaviors associated with running away. This study also sought to determine a predictive equation by comparing a group of adolescent runaways to two other criterion groups: a maladjusted sample and a control sample. In addition, it was hypothesized that there would be differences between the samples and that selected variables would distinguish between the groups.

An overview of the history of adolescent runaway behavior indicates that it has become a social and psychological problem of significant proportions. Estimates of runaway behavior range from 2 to 4 million per year with approximately three percent of American families experiencing a runaway episode each year (Garbarino, 1986).

Runaway behavior has been defined as a behavioral manifestation of psychopathology. Recent research has indicated that this behavior has become more indicative of psychopathology than previously thought (Norey & Donohue, 1985). However, very little of the recent research had used a typical standardized personality assessment instrument that was representative of the apparent psychopathology associated with the adolescent runaway. The National Network of Runaway and Youth Services (1985) survey indicated that the most frequently cited presenting problems of runaway youth were: depression, alcohol usage, drug usage, physical abuse, sexual abuse, suicidal tendencies, and severe psychological problems. The research that discriminated runaways from non-runaways and also had reported classification rates measured discriminate variables such as: self-esteem and perceptions of parental positivity (Englander, 1984); peer relationships, parents' marital relationship and family constellation (Gilchrist, 1984); school problems, neglect, abuse, bad influences (Barber & Hosch, 1983); and delinquency (Linden, 1980). A review of runaway research also indicated that there were methodological problems, and that conceptualization of the runaway phenomenon as a holistic personality syndrome had not been presented. Evidence of a personality assessment instrument that was representative of the behaviors characteristic of running away and had discriminatory power was needed.

Sample. Three sample groups were used in the investigation. The runaway sample was composed of the residents who resided at the Memphis, Tennessee Family Link/Runaway House between 1986 and 1988 and whose custodian (primarily female) completed the Personality Inventory for Children - Revised. The total runaway sample was 61.

The control sample consisted of 60 adolescent subjects, male and female, age 13 through 17. The subjects were members of various church youth groups and had never run away from home nor had seen a mental health professional.

The maladjusted sample was a random sample of 59 PIC-R protocols of maladjusted adolescents aged 13 through 17. These 59 protocols were from a larger sample of 1226 subjects seen at an outpatient clinic in Detroit, Michigan for problematic behavioral and emotional adjustment. All the subjects in this sample had DSM-III diagnoses. However, for the purposes of this study, any subjects who had the diagnosis of conduct disorder were excluded from this sample because one of the criteria for the diagnosis of conduct disorder is running away. To eliminate this possible confounding variable, those subjects were not used as part of the random sample.

Design and analysis. This study used an ex post facto design. Selected variables, which were scales of the PIC-R, were used to determine if, in a linear combination, they could discriminate between the criterion groups: an adolescent control sample, an adolescent maladjusted sample, and an adolescent runaway sample. The discriminating variables were: Adjustment, Achievement, Depression, Family Relationships, Delinquency, and Social Skills. Discriminate analysis was used to accomplish this study.

Instrument. The standardized personality measure used in this study was the short form of the Personality Inventory for Children - Revised. It is a 280, true-false item personality inventory with 16 profile scales plus four factor scales. One screening scale and five clinical scales were used because they represented the characteristics associated with adolescent runaway behavior. Those scales were: Adjustment, Achievement, Depression, Family Relationships, Delinquency, and Social Skills, respectively.

Research questions. This study addressed two research questions:

1. Could male runaways be discriminated from a male control sample and a male maladjusted sample on a personality inventory?

2. Could female runaways be discriminated from a female control sample and a female maladjusted sample on a personality inventory?

Hypotheses and findings. Three null hypotheses were generated from the research questions. The hypotheses and related findings were as follows:

Ho1: There is no difference between males and females, on selected personality scales of the Personality Inventory for Children - Revised (Adjustment, Achievement, Depression, Family Relations, Delinquency, Social Skills), within a sample of adolescent runaways, a maladjusted adolescent sample, and a control sample.

A multivariate analysis of variance (MANOVA) was used to determine if there were significant differences ($p < .05$) within each group due to gender. These results indicated that within each of the three criterion groups (control, runaway, and maladjusted) on each scale there was not a significant difference ($p > .05$) between the male and female subjects. Analysis also indicated that between the three groups there were significant differences ($p < .05$). This difference was probably due to the combining of the three groups and due to the control group's lower mean scores.

Due to there being no significant differences between male and female subjects within each of the three criterion groups, the male and female subjects in each group were merged. The null hypothesis was therefore rejected.

Ho2: There is no difference on selected personality scales of the Personality Inventory for Children - Revised (Adjustment, Achievement, Depression, Family Relations, Delinquency, Social Skills) among a sample of adolescent runaways, a maladjusted adolescent sample, and an adolescent control sample.

A one-way analysis of variance and Scheffe's post-hoc analysis indicated the following: that the control sample was significantly different ($p < .05$) from the runaway and maladjusted samples and that the runaway and maladjusted samples were not significantly different ($p > .05$) from each other on the variables Adjustment, Depression, Family Relations, and Social Skills, but significantly different (p < .05) on the Delinquency variable. The second null hypothesis was therefore rejected.

The findings of the analysis of the first two hypotheses indicated that it was expeditious to combine the runaway and maladjusted samples and calculate a step-wise discriminate analysis in order to try and predict membership into one of two groups, a control sample or a runaway/maladjusted sample.

Ho3: The Personality Inventory for Children - Revised variables (Adjustment, Achievement, Depression, Family Relations, Delinquency, Social Skills) will not predict membership in one of two groups, a control sample or a runaway/maladjusted sample.

The results of the step-wise discriminate analysis indicated that five variables, Adjustment, Family Relations, Depression, Delinquency, and Social Skills, significantly distinguished (p < .05) between the two criterion groups. In addition, cross-validation application of the discriminate function also significantly predicted criterion group membership. The third null hypothesis was therefore rejected.

CONCLUSIONS

The purpose of this study was to use a personality measure that was representative of a cluster of behaviors associated with running away and to determine a predictive equation by comparing a group of adolescent runaways to two other criterion groups: a maladjusted (psychiatric) sample and a control sample whose subjects had not run away nor had ever been referred to a mental health professional for psychological problems.

Adolescent runaway personality profile. Five scales of the PIC-R were found that are predictive variables representative of the behaviors associated with adolescent runaways. While the literature on adolescent runaway behavior had been discordant in its presentation and representation of runaway behavior, these five predictive variables have been able to discriminate between a runaway sample, a maladjusted sample, and a control sample. An interpretation of the corresponding mean scores associated with the predictive variables (scales) is necessary in order to conceptualize runaway behavior as a personality profile.

Lachar and Gdowski (1979) have developed an actuarial system designed to render interpretative hypotheses or rather assign behavioral correlates to PIC-R T-scores. The actuarial assessment system is essentially a "cook-book" approach to the interpretation to the PIC-R. Differing behavioral correlates are associated with ranges of scores. For instance, with the Adjustment scale the same interpretation is given to any scale score 60 and above. Whereas, with the Delinquency scale differing interpretations are given to scale scores between 80-89T, 90-99T, greater than 99T and greater than 109T. By applying this PIC actuarial system to the derived scale scores, via the tested hypotheses, a personality profile of the adolescent runaway evidences itself when compared to a control sample and a runaway/maladjusted sample.

Adjustment. When interpreting the PIC-R, the Adjustment scale is used as a psychological screening measure (see Appendix B) for identifying children who are in need of psychological evaluation. Since the runaway sample and the maladjusted sample were not significantly different (p < .05) from each other they received the same actuarial interpretation:

> The description of this child's behavior suggests that a psychological/psychiatric evaluation may assist in the remediation of current problems. (Lachar & Gdowski, 1979, p. 90)

If psychopathology is present, as Riemer (1940), Jenkins (1969) and National Network of Runaway Youth Services (1985) believe, then a psychological/psychiatric evaluation is indicated.

Achievement. The Achievement scale was developed to assist in identifying children whose academic achievement was below expectancy. On this scale, the runaway and maladjusted samples were not significantly different (p < .05) and received the same actuarial interpretation:

> Inventory responses suggest the possibility of poor school performance and associated academic retardation; teacher observation of limited concentration and difficulty in completion of classroom assignments may be associated with below age expectation performance in reading, mathematics, or spelling. (Lachar & Gdowski, 1979, p. 90)

This outcome and interpretation is consistent with Phillip's (1976) findings that the runaway repeater girl has a pattern of repeated grade retention and low achievement, and this study indicates boys evidence the same pattern.

Depression. The Depression scale reflects childhood depression. Since the runaway sample and the maladjusted sample were not significantly different (p < .05) from each other, they received the same actuarial interpretation:

> Similar children are often described as sad or unhappy; their
> dispositions are often characterized by frequent mood changes
> which may occur without apparent cause; frequent periods of
> crying or isolation may be characteristic. (Lachar & Gdowski,
> 1979, p. 93)

This outcome and interpretation supports the National Network of
Runaway Youth Services (1985) survey indicating that the primary
presenting problem was depression. That runaways are depressed was also
found by Scalf (1978).

Family relations. The Family Relations scale reflects a measure of
family effectiveness and cohesion. Since the runaway sample and the
maladjusted sample were not significantly different ($p < .05$) from each
other, they received the same actuarial interpretation:

> The home is likely to reflect the impact of divorce or
> separation and may be characterized by instability and
> conflict; parental inconsistency in setting limits is suggested;
> the resulting parent/child interactions may contribute to the
> development of child behavior problems. (Lachar & Gdowski,
> 1979, p. 94)

Ackerman's (1980) findings of the home being disrupted due to death,
divorce, or separation, and Adler's (1980) finding that adolescent
runaways felt rejected by their parents was supported by this study's
findings. This study further supports Blood & D'Angelo's (1974) finding
that adolescent runaways believe their home to be conflictual and
intolerable.

Social skills. The Social Skills scale measures the various
characteristics that reflect effective social relations in childhood. On this
scale, while significant differences ($p < .05$) occurred, the mean scores for
the groups were low and not actuarially interpretable (Lachar & Gdowski,
1979). That is, a statistical difference ($p < .05$) was found, but the scores
did not achieve the cutoff point which would yield an actuarial
interpretation. Therefore, because the Social Skills scale could not be
interpreted, it is not included in the personality profile of the adolescent
runaway.

Delinquency. The Delinquency scale was developed to measure the
behavior characteristics of delinquents and to be a diagnostic aid in
identifying delinquent children. While both the runaway and maladjusted
samples were significantly different ($p < .05$) from the control sample,
they were also significantly different ($p < .05$) from each other. The

runaway sample had a higher mean score than the maladjusted sample. The Delinquency subscale illustrates a distinct difference between the runaway and maladjusted samples. The actuarial interpretation for the runaway and maladjusted samples were the same initially. This is because, higher cut-off scores subsume the interpretive behavioral correlates of the lower cut-off scores. On this scale the runaway sample had a higher cut-off score making it similar to the maladjusted sample for interpretive purposes:

> A disregard for rules and societal expectation is likely to be evidenced by behavior displayed at both home and school; similar children may express a dislike for school and demonstrate a hostile, defiant response to school personnel; current behavior is likely to reflect impulsivity, poor judgment or unmodulated hostility; an antisocial adjustment may be suggested by such symptoms as lying, stealing, associated with similar troubled children, or by an established tendency to blame others for current problems. (Lachar & Gdowski, 1979, p.95)

However, since the runaway sample had a higher cut-off score, this sample has an additional actuarial interpretation which distinguishes the runaway sample from the maladjusted sample:

> A characterological disorder may be suggested by such symptoms as lying, stealing, problematic sexual behavior and group delinquent activities. (Lachar & Gdowski, 1979, p. 95)

Other researchers (Riemer, 1940; Blood & D'Angelo, 1974; and Linden, 1980) have found delinquent type behaviors associated with adolescent runaways. Edelbrock (1980) found stealing outside the home was associated with adolescent runaways. School behavior problems (Gutierres & Reich, 1981) and truancy and negative attitudes toward school (Nye, 1980) were consistent findings of runaways. Previous research is supportive of this study's findings that a characterological disorder is associated with adolescent runaways.

In summary, what distinguishes the adolescent runaway from a maladjusted adolescent (psychiatric outpatient) is that the runaway may have a character disorder while the maladjusted youth does not. The American Psychiatric Association (1975) defines character disorder as:

> A personality disorder manifested by a chronic and habitual pattern of reaction that is maladaptive in that it is relatively inflexible, limits the optimal use of potentialities, and often provokes the very counter-reaction from the environment that the subject wishes to avoid. (p. 31)

The possible presence of a personality disorder, which distinguishes the runaway sample from the maladjusted sample, is indicative of a serious psychopathology. This finding is consistent with the National Network of Runaway Youth Services (1985) survey finding that a severe psychological problem is one of the presenting problems of runaway youth.

While the predictive validity of the five variables in linear combination was objectively verified by the 96.83% rate of correct classification and the cross-validation 93.02% rate of correct classification, some caution should be used in generalizing these findings. Random sampling did not occur for all three groups; thus external validity may be compromised. Generalizing these findings to other groups should reflect this limitation.

Summary. The findings of this study indicate that the PIC-R is an extremely effective personality measure. This instrument's ability to conceptually represent the behavior and personality problems of runaway adolescents is excellent. Its utility is further enhanced by its sensitivity in discriminating criterion groups. This sensitivity is exceptional because of the actuarial interpretive system associated with this instrument. The refinement of this instrument, due to the actuarial interpretive system, is what enables the PIC-R to detect the presence or not of psychopathology.

RECOMMENDATIONS

The findings in this study support several recommendations.

1. The PIC-R, as a personality measure, is extremely reflective of the behaviors associated with adolescent runaways. Its power to discriminate the presence of psychopathology or not is indicative of its usefulness to runaway programs. The findings of this research indicate that psychopathology was present in runaways tested in this study. Based on this finding, an in-house psychological assessment using the PIC-R procedure should be developed to enhance treatment plan formulation. This diagnostic service could greatly enhance professional credibility - especially for referral purposes.

2. The survey by the National Network of Runaway and Youth Services (1985) indicated that the runaway shelters are seeing more youth with more mental health problems than previously. The PIC-R provides validity to the survey's findings. It is recommended that, since more psychologically disturbed youth are seeking services at runaway programs

and that since the PIC-R is able to detect psychopathology in the runaway adolescent, mental health services be provided to the adolescent and his/her family on the agency's premises (Chwast, 1978). It is recommended that these runaway programs consider hiring trained mental health professionals due to the mental health problems likely to be encountered in such settings. In general, current typical runaway program staff do not possess these qualifications. If mental health services are provided by less qualified agency staff, the agency runs the risk of malpractice by misdiagnosing, not providing qualified practitioners, and not providing appropriate treatment programs. If in-house services cannot be provided then the programs should network with community mental health resources, both public and private, in order to meet the youth's mental health needs.

3. Mental health services provided to adolescents can be conceptualized on a least-to-most-restrictive continuum: outpatient mental health services, day treatment programs (partial-hospitalization), and psychiatric (inpatient) hospitalization. Access to the different services is, at least, dependent upon diagnosis of psychopathology. Results obtained from PIC-R runaway profiles indicates that some runaway's psychological profiles can be classified or typed into a mental health outpatient group (Lachar, 1990). Taxonomic or typological systems on runaways have been historically inadequate. Prior taxonomic systems have been criticized for the following reasons: (1) The researchers used an "intuitive" based approach rather than an objective statistical multivariate taxonomic method; (2) The samples have been extremely limited, small, and basically nonrepresentative; (3) The "descriptive domain" has been narrow; researchers use different sets of variables and therefore reach a different taxonomic system; and (4) The systems have not been validated or tested for reliability (Brennan et al., 1978). A typology or taxonomic system on runaways is suggested here that is based upon the degree of psychopathology present. The adolescent runaway's mental health needs could be met by one of the providers on the continuum of mental health services. Adolescent runaways are classified or typed based upon the mental health services required; either outpatient services, day treatment services, or inpatient hospitalization services. Concomitant with this taxonomic system is that much effort needs to be placed in the area of diagnosing adolescent runaways.

4. Future research should include the use of discriminant analysis with additional comparison groups to investigate the utility of the suggested typology based upon the continuum of services. This research should focus on the continued use of the PIC-R in establishing personality profiles of select criterion groups. These criterion groups should represent

the common presenting problems that were found in the survey by the National Network of Runaway Youth Services (1985). The criterion groups are depressed/non-suicidal, depressed/suicidal, physically abused, sexually abused, alcohol and drug dependant, and investigate completely "severe psychological problems". The criterion group, "severe psychological problems", could be operationally defined as those runaways who have been admitted to psychiatric inpatient hospitals immediately following a runaway episode.

Appendix A

Personality Inventory for Children Scales

Adjustment (ADJ): This scale was developed as a screening measure to identify children who are in need of a psychological evaluation and as a general measure of poor psychological adjustment. The scale score-to-criterion validity index was .76 and with a correct classification of 88.5%.

Achievement (ACH): This scale was developed to assist in the identification of children who's academic achievement is significantly below age expectation regardless of intellectual capacity. The scale score-to-criterion validity index was .79 and with a correct classification of 92% with a cross validation sample.

Depression (D): This scale is an inventory of items judged by experienced clinicians to reflect childhood depression. The Childhood Depression Inventory (Kovaks & Beck, 1977) correlated significantly with parental report on the PIC D scale ($r = .33$, $p < .05$).

Family Relations (FAM): A scale containing items judged to measure family effectiveness and cohesion. Snyder (1981) concluded that FAM elevations can signal, within the context of an assessment of a child, the need for detailed evaluation of marital interaction and may suggest the desirability of marital counseling.

Delinquency (DLQ): This scale was developed to be a concurrent measure of the behavioral characteristics manifest by delinquents and a diagnostic aid in the identification of delinquent children. The scale score-to-criterion validity was .89 with a cross validation sample. A classification ruled correctly identified 97% of construction sample delinquents.

Social Skills (SSK): This scale measures the various characteristics that reflect effective social relations in childhood: ability to leave and to follow, level of active participation in organized activities, self confidence and poise in social situations, and comprehension and tact and interpersonal relations. Kurdek & Krile (1983) found that SSK correlated significantly with a self report measure of social competence ($r = -.33$, $p < .001$).

RELIABILITY

Three studies were conducted to assess the stability of the PIC scales. The first study had an interval between testing of approximately 51 days. The reliability coefficient was .71. The second study had an interval of 15 days. The reliability coefficient was .86. The third study had an interval of 14 days. The reliability coefficient was .89.

The internal consistency was assessed and coefficient alpha estimates on 13 scales ranged from .57 to .86 with a mean alpha of .76.

Appendix B
ANOVA Results for Religious Affiliation by PIC Scales

TABLE 1

ANOVA RESULTS FOR RELIGIOUS AFFILIATION BY ADJUSTMENT SCALE

Source of Variation	DF	SS	MS	F
Religious Affiliation	4	375.7079	93.9270	1.1393
Error	55	4534.2254	82.4405	
Total	59	4909.9333		

Group	Count	M	SD
Jewish	21	51.2857	11.1317
Episcopal	7	48.7143	4.8206
Baptist	18	47.2778	8.1515
Unclassified	10	50.1000	4.9542
Methodist/Catholic/ Presbyterian	4	57.0000	13.7356
Total	60	49.9667	9.1225

TABLE 2
ANOVA RESULTS FOR RELIGIOUS AFFILIATION BY ACHIEVEMENT SCALE

Source of Variation	DF	SS	MS	F
Religious Affiliation	4	294.5619	73.6405	.6714
Error	55	6032.8381	109.6880	
Total	59	6327.4000		

Group	Count	M	SD
Jewish	21	45.4762	9.1193
Episcopal	7	41.0000	8.8694
Baptist	18	46.5000	1.7986
Unclassified	10	49.3000	0.5415
Methodist/Catholic/ Presbyterian	4	45.5006	3.3041
Total	60	45.9000	0.3559

TABLE 6
~~OVA~~ RESULTS FOR RELIGIOUS AFFILIATION BY SOCIAL SKILLS SCALE

Source of Variation	DF	SS	MS	F
Religious Affiliation	4	167.7681	41.9413	.3678
Error	55	6271.5683	114.0285	
Total	59	6439.3333		

Group	Count	M	SD
Jewish	21	43.5714	10.9616
Episcopal	7	45.5714	11.2673
Baptist	18	41.7778	11.4098
Unclassified	10	44.2000	9.1627
Methodist/Catholic/ Presbyterian	4	48.0000	6.7823
Total	60	43.6667	10.4471

TABLE 3
ANOVA RESULTS FOR RELIGIOUS AFFILIATION BY DEPRESSION SCALE

Source of Variation	DF	SS	MS	F
Religious Affiliation	4	827.3071	206.8268	2.4195*
Error	55	4701.5429	85.4826	
Total	59	5528.8500		

Group	Count	M	SD
Jewish	21	52.7143	9.0063
Episcopal	7	50.8571	1.8241
Baptist	18	47.6667	7.9926
Unclassified	10	51.4000	10.8955
Methodist/Catholic/ Presbyterian	4	63.0000	5.3541
Total	60	51.4500	9.6804

*p<.05

TABLE 4
ANOVA RESULTS FOR RELIGIOUS AFFILIATION BY FAMILY RELATIONS SCALE

Source of Variation	DF	SS	MS	F
Religious Affiliation	4	44.3198	11.0800	.1741
Error	55	3499.3302	63.6242	
Total	59	3543.6500		

Group	Count	M	SD
Jewish	21	49.8571	7.9201
Episcopal	7	47.4286	5.6231
Baptist	18	48.5556	8.6855
Unclassified	10	48.8000	8.6384
Methodist/Catholic/ Presbyterian	4	47.5000	5.8023
Total	60	48.8500	7.7500

TABLE 5
ANOVA RESULTS FOR RELIGIOUS
DELINQUENCY SC...

Source of Variation	DF	SS
Religious Affiliation	4	247.7595
Error	55	4060.4238
Total	59	4308.1833

Group	Cou...
Jewish	21
Episcopal	7
Baptist	18
Unclassified	10
Methodist/Catholic/ Presbyterian	4
Total	60

Appendix C

Two-Way ANOVA Results for Age Groups by PIC Scales

TABLE 1
TWO-WAY ANOVA FOR AGE GROUPS BY
ADJUSTMENT SCALE

Source of Variation	SS	DF	MS	F
Criterion Group	54689.601	2	27344.801	156.822*
Age Group	205.813	1	205.813	1.180
CGRP by AGRP	327.215	2	163.607	.938
ERROR	30340.159	174	174.366	

*p<.05

TABLE 2
TWO-WAY ANOVA FOR AGE GROUPS BY
ACHIEVEMENT SCALE

Source of Variation	SS	DF	MS	F
Criterion				
Group	10410.671	2	5205.336	37.107*
Age Group	299.522	1	299.522	2.135
CGRP by AGRP	57.697	2	28.849	.206
ERROR	24408.375	174	140.278	

*p<.05

TABLE 3
TWO-WAY ANOVA FOR AGE GROUPS BY
DEPRESSION SCALE

Source of Variation	SS	DF	MS	F
Criterion				
Group	15644.242	2	7822.121	51.295*
Age Group	85.692	1	85.692	.562
CGRP by AGRP	56.764	2	28.382	.186
ERROR	26533.844	174	152.493	

*p<.05

TABLE 4
TWO-WAY ANOVA FOR AGE GROUPS BY FAMILY RELATIONS SCALE

Source of Variation	SS	DF	MS	F
Criterion				
Group	7585.975	2	3792.988	35.771*
Age Group	29.757	1	29.757	.281
CGRP by AGRP	5.618	2	2.809	.026
ERROR	18450.150	174	106.035	

*p<.05

TABLE 5
TWO-WAY ANOVA FOR AGE GROUPS BY DELINQUENCY SCALE

Source of Variation	SS	DF	MS	F
Criterion				
Group	93031.514	2	46515.757	191.532*
Age Group	22.862	1	22.862	.094
CGRP by AGRP	309.265	2	154.633	.637
ERROR	42257.965	174	242.862	

*p<.05

TABLE 6

TWO-WAY ANOVA FOR AGE GROUPS BY SOCIAL SKILLS SCALE

Source of Variation	SS	DF	MS	F
Criterion				
Group	18872.620	2	9346.310	59.518*
Age Group	.792	1	.792	.005
CGRP by AGRP	69.950	2	34.975	.221
ERROR	27586.955	174	158.546	

*p<.05

Appendix D

Univariate F-Tests for Groups by Sex

TABLE 1
UNIVARIATE F-TESTS FOR GROUPS BY SEX

Variable	Sum of Squares	Error Sum of Squares	Hypoth. Mean Square	Error Mean Square	F
ADJ	1184.44	26763.48	592.22	164.19	3.61*
ACH	124.98	20472.19	62.49	125.60	.50
DEP	316.61	24603.44	158.30	150.94	1.05
FAM	50.97	14390.81	25.49	88.29	.29
DLQ	237.83	38118.76	233.91	233.86	.51
SSK	351.64	24551.61	175.82	250.62	1.17

* $p < .05$

Appendix E

ANOVA Results and Scheffé Test for Groups
by
PIC Scales

TABLE 1
ANOVA RESULTS FOR GROUPS BY ADJUSTMENT
SCALE

Source of Variation	DF	DD	MS	F
Criterion Group				
Between Groups	2	54886.71	27443.35	158.88*
Within Groups	166	28671.95	172.72	
Total	168	83558.67		

< .05

TABLE 2
SCHEFFE' TEST FOR ADJUSTMENT SCALE

Group	Count	Mean	Comparison Groups	S
Control-1	59	49.62	1,2 = 39.17 > .03*	
Runaway-2	57	88.80	1,3 = 36.14 > .14*	
Maladjusted-3	53	85.77	2,3 = 3.03 < 6.20	

* p < .05

TABLE 3
ANOVA RESULTS FOR GROUPS BY ACHIEVEMENT
SCALE

Source of Variation	DF F	SS	MS
Between Groups	2 41.46*	10607.58	5303.79
Within Groups	166	21233.35	127.91
Total	168	31840.94	

* p < .05

TABLE 4
SCHEFFE' TEST FOR ACHIEVEMENT SCALE

Group	Count	Mean	Comparison Groups		S
Control-1 5.19*	59	45.23	1,2 = 15.41	>	
Runaway-2 5.29*	57	60.64	1,3 = 17.68	>	
Maladjusted-3 5.33	53	62.92	2,3 = 2.27	<	

* $p < .05$

TABLE 5
ANOVA RESULTS FOR GROUPS BY DEPRESSION SCALE

Source of Variation	DF	SS	MS	F
Between Groups 52.22*	2	15701.74	7850.87	
Within Groups	166	24953.85	150.32	
Total	168	40655.60		

* $p < .05$

TABLE 6
SCHEFFE' TEST FOR DEPRESSION SCALE

Group	Count	Mean	Comparison Groups	S
Control-1 5.63*	59	51.54	1,2 = 19.87	>
Runaway-2 5.73*	57	71.42	1,3 = 20.57	>
Maladjusted-3 5.78	53	72.11	2,3 = .69	<

* $p < .05$

TABLE 7
ANOVA RESULTS FOR GROUPS BY FAMILY RELATIONS SCALE

Source of Variation	DF	SS	MS	F
Between Groups	2	7439.39	3719.69	42.15*
Within Groups	166	14648.60	88.24	
Total	168	22088.00		

* $p < .05$

TABLE 8
SCHEFFE' TEST FOR FAMILY RELATIONS SCALE

Group	Count	Mean	Comparison Groups	S
Control-1 4.31*	59	48.50	1,2 = 12.54	>
Runaway-2 4.39*	57	61.05	1,3 = 15.05	>
Maladjusted-3 4.43	53	63.56	2,3 = 2.51	<

* $p < .05$

TABLE 9
ANOVA RESULTS FOR GROUPS BY DELINQUENCY
SCALE

Source of Variation	DF	SS	MS	F
Between Groups	2	91415.25	45707.62	197.36*
Within Groups	166	38443.12	231.58	
Total	168	129858.37		

* $p < .05$

TABLE 10
SCHEFFE' TEST FOR DELINQUENCY SCALE

Group	Count	Mean	Comparison Groups	S
Control-1	59	50.00	1,2 = 52.73	>
6.98*				
Runaway-2	57	102.73	1,3 = 43.13	>
7.11*				
Maladjusted-3	53	93.13	2,3 = 9.60	>
7.17*				

* $p < .05$

TABLE 11
ANOVA RESULTS FOR GROUPS BY SOCIAL SKILLS
SCALE

Source of Variation	DF	SS	MS	F
Between Groups	2	20354.32	10177.16	67.83*
Within Groups	166	24903.42	150.02	
Total	168	45257.75		

* $p < .05$

TABLE 12
SCHEFFE' TEST FOR SOCIAL SKILLS SCALE

Group	Count	Mean	Comparison Groups	S	
Control-1	59	43.27	1,2 = 21.88	>	5.62*
Runaway-2	57	65.15	1,3 = 24.08	>	5.72*
Maladjusted-3	53	67.35	2,3 = 2.20	<	5.77

* p < .05

Bibliography

Ackerman, R. J. (1980). "The effects of parent death, long term illness, and divorce on children running away from home" (Doctoral dissertation, Western Michigan University, 1980). *Dissertation Abstracts International*, 41, 8231A.

Adams, G. R. & Munro, G. (1979). "Portrait of the North American runaway: A critical review." *Journal of Youth and Adolescence*, 8, 359-373.

Adler, I. S. (1980). "A profile of the runaway prone adolescent girl and a psychodiagnostic instrument for her detection." (Doctoral dissertation, University of California, Los Angeles, 1979). *Dissertation Abstracts International*, 40, 3914B.

American Psychiatric Association (1987). *Diagnostic and statistical manual of mental disorders* (3rd ed, rev). Washington, DC: Author.

American Psychiatric Association (1975). *A psychiatric glossary (4th ed.)*. New York: Basic Books, Inc.

Arulanandam, S. J. (1980). "Runaway adolescents perception of their parental behavior and environment" (Doctoral dissertation, Loyola University of Chicago, 1980). *Dissertation Abstracts International*, 41, 1562B.

Barber, A. V., & Hosch, H. M. (1983). "Development and Evaluation of the Barber Inventory of Runaway Determinants." Unpublished manuscript.

Blood, L., & D'Angelo, R. (1974). "A progress research report on value issues in conflict between runaways and their parents." *Journal of Marriage and the Family*, 36, 486-490.

Brandon, J. S. (1975). "The relationship of runaway behavior in adolescents to the individuals perceptions of self, the environment, and parental antecedents" (Doctoral dissertation, University of Maryland, 1975). *Dissertation Abstracts International*, 36, 646B.

Brennan, T., Hiuzinga, D., & Elliott, S. S. (1978). *The social psychology of runaways*. Lexington Massachusetts: D. P. Heath and Company.

Brown, D. T. (1985). "Review of the Millon Adolescent Personality Inventory." In J. V. Mitchell, Jr. (Ed.). *Ninth Mental Measurements Yearbook* (pp. 978-979). Lincoln: The University of Nebraska Press.

Burke, W. H. (1985). "Runaway youth: An analysis of personality and psychological characteristics" (Doctoral dissertation, The

Florida State University, 1985). *Dissertation Abstracts International*, 46, 2923A.

Buros, O. (Ed). (1972). *Seventh Mental Measurements Yearbook.* Lincoln: The University of Nebraska Press.

Busch-Rossnagel, N. A. (1985). "Review of the Family Environment Scale." In J. V. Mitchell, Jr. (Ed.). *Ninth Mental Measurements Yearbook* (pp. 573-574). Lincoln: The University of Nebraska Press.

Butt, D. S. (1978). "Review of the Jesness Inventory." In O. Buros (Ed.). *Eighth Mental Measurements Yearbook* (pp. 876-878). Lincoln: The University of Nebraska Press.

Chwast, R. (1977). "Psychotherapy of disadvantaged acting-out adolescents." *American Journal of Psychotherapy*, 31, 216-226.

Doty, S. A. (1979). "Runaway behavior and perceived resource availability in adolescent females" (Doctoral dissertation, University of Texas at Austin, 1979). *Dissertation Abstracts International*, 41, 1332B.

Dreyer, P. H. (1978). "Review of the Family Environment Scale." In O. Buros (Ed.). *Eighth Mental Measurements Yearbook* (pp. 820-821). Lincoln: The University of Nebraska Press.

Edelbrock, C. (1980). "Running away from home: Incidents and correlates among children and youth referred for mental health services." *Journal of Family Issues*, 1, 210-228.

Englander, S. W. (1984). "Some self-reported correlates of runaway behavior in adolescent females." *Journal of Consulting and Clinical Psychology*, 52, 484-485.

Forbes, G. B. (1986). "Comparison of the short and original scales of the Personality Inventory for Children." *Journal of Clinical Psychology*, 42, 129-132.

Freudenberger, H. J., & Torkelsen, S. E. (1984). "Beyond the interpersonal: a systems model of therapeutic care for homeless children and youth." *Psychotherapy*, 21, 132-140.

Fry, P. S. (1982). "Paternal correlates of adolescent runaway behavior: Implications for adolescent development and considerations for intervention and treatment of adolescent runaways." *Journal of Applied Developmental Psychology*, 3, 347-360.

Garbarino, J., Schellenback, C., & Sebes, J. (Ed.). (1986). *Troubled youth, troubled families.* Aldine de Gruyter.

Gilchrist, L. (1984). "Use of the Revised Self-Administering Lifestyle Inventory in distinguishing between runaway and non-runaway adolescents" (Doctoral dissertation, Idaho State University, 1984). *Dissertation Abstracts International*, 45, 3071A.

Gullotta, T. P. (1979). "Leaving home: Family relationships of the runaway child." *Social Casework*, 60, 111-114.

Gutierres, S. E. & Reich, J. W. (1981). "A developmental perspective on runaway behavior: Its relationship to child abuse." *Child Welfare*, 60, 89-94.

Harris, L. H. (1980). "Middle-class high school dropouts: Incidence of physical abuse, incest, sexual assault, loss, symptomatic behavior, and emotional disturbance" (Doctoral dissertation, University of Minnesota, 1980). *Dissertation Abstracts International*, 41, 2058A.

Hogan, R. (1972). "Review of the High School Personality Questionnaire." In O. Buros (Ed.). *Seventh Mental Measurements Yearbook* (pp. 207-208). Lincoln: The University of Nebraska Press.

Hughes, K. A. (1981). "The reported incidence of incest among runaway female adolescents" (Doctoral dissertation, California School of Professional Psychology, Berkeley, 1980). *Dissertation Abstracts International*, 41, 4638B.

Jackson, D. N. (1972). "Review of the High School Personality Questionnaire." In O. Buros (Ed.). *Seventh Mental Measurements Yearbook* (pp. 209-211). Lincoln: The University of Nebraska Press.

Jenkins, R. L. (1969). "Classification of behavior problems of children." *American Journal of Psychiatry*, 125, 1032-1039.

Johnson, N. S., & Peck, R. (1978). "Sibship composition and the adolescent runaway phenomenon." *Journal of Youth and Adolescence*, 7, 301-305.

Klecka, W.R. (1980). *Discriminant Analysis*. Beverly Hills: Sage Publications, Inc.

Lachar, D. (1982). *Personality Inventory for Children (PIC): Revised Format Manual Supplement.* Los Angeles: Western Psychological Services.

Lachar, D. (1990). "Adolescent outpatient data set of PIC-R profiles". Unpublished data.

Lachar, D. (1984). *Multidimensional Description of Child Personality: A manual for the Personality Inventory for Children.* Los Angeles: Western Psychological Services.

Lachar, D. & Gdowski, C.L. (1979). "Problem behavior factor correlates of Personality Inventory for Children Profile

Scales." *Journal of Consulting and Clinical Psychology*, 47, 39-48.

Lachar, D., Gdowski, C.L. & Snyder, D.K. (1984). "External validation of the Personality Inventory for Children (PIC) Profile and Factor Scales: Parent, teacher, and clinician Ratings." *Journal of Consulting and Clinical Psychology*, 52, 155-164.

Linden, B. W. (1979). "Personality characteristics, family variables, and ego - development in runaway girls" (Doctoral dissertation, University of Wyoming, 1979). *Dissertation Abstracts International*, 41, 694B.

Maar, J. E. (1984). "Critical factors related to adolescent runaway behavior in the state of Florida" (Doctoral dissertation, The Florida State University, 1984). *Dissertation Abstracts International*, 45, 2993A.

Mitchell, J. & Dodder, R. A. (1980). "An examination of types of delinquency through path analysis." *Journal of Youth and Adolescence*, 9, 239-248.

Moriarity, D. T. (1975). "Runaways: Psychological and sociological study" (Doctoral dissertation, United States International University, 1975). *Dissertation Abstracts International*, 36, 496B.

National Network of Runaway and Youth Services, Inc. (1985). *A profile of America's runaway and homeless youth and the programs that help them.* Washington, DC: Author.

Norey, D. M. & Donohue, S. (1985). "The relationship between adolescent life stress events and delinquent conduct including conduct indicating a need for supervision." *Adolescence*, 20, 313-321.

Nye, F. I. "Runaways: Some critical issues for professionals in society". *Cooperative Extension Bulletin - 0744*, Washington State University, 1980.

Olson, L. R. (1977). "Suburban runaways: A follow up study" (Doctoral dissertation, University of Maryland, 1977). *Dissertation Abstracts International*, 38, 2379B.

Olson, L., Liebow, E., Mannino, F. V., & Shore, M. F. (1980). "Runaway children twelve years later: A follow up." *Journal of Family Issues*, 1, 165-188.

Phillips, S. B. (1976). "The runaway girl: A differentiating profile of personality, family, school and social factors" (Doctoral dissertation, Rutgers University, 1978). *Dissertation Abstracts International*, 39, 394B.

Pipp, F. D. (1979). "Actuarial analysis of adolescent personality: Self-report correlates for the Personality Inventory for Children profile scales." *Unpublished masters thesis,* Wayne State University, Detroit, Michigan.

Riemer, M. (1940). "Runaway children." *American Journal of Orthopsychiatry,* 10, 522-527.

Roberts, A. R. (1982a). "Stress and coping patterns among adolescent runaways." *Journal of Social Service Research,* 5, 15-27.

Robins, L. N. (1958) "Mental illness of the runaway: A 30-year follow-up study." *Human Organization,* 16, 1-15.

Robins, L. N., & O'Neal, P. (1959). "The adult prognosis for runaway children." *American Journal of Orthopsychiatry,* 29, 752-761.

Satchell, M. (1986, July 20). "Kids for sale." *Parade Magazine,* pp. 3-6.

Scalf, L. D. (1978). "Self-esteem of the runaway" (Doctoral Dissertation, The Florida State University, 1978). *Dissertation Abstracts International,* 39, 2967B.

Shavelson, R. J. (1981). *Statistical reasoning for the behavioral sciences.* Boston: Allyn and Bacon, Inc.

Sines, J. O. (1978). "Review of the Family Environment Scale." In O. Buros (Ed.). *Eighth Mental Measurements Yearbook* (pp. 822-823). Lincoln: The University of Nebraska Press.

Spillane-Greico, E. (1984). "Characteristics of a helpful relationship: A study of empathic understanding and positive regard between runaways and their parents." *Adolescence,* 19, 63-75.

Steinbock, L. A. (1977). "Nest leaving: Family systems of runaway adolescents" (Doctoral dissertation, 1978). *Dissertation Abstracts International,* 38, 4544B.

Sweeney, K. M. (1976). "A comparison study of parental attitudes of parents of runaway teenagers and parents of non-runaway teenagers." Unpublished manuscript, United States International University.

Sweetland, R. C. & Keyser, D. J. (1986). *Tests: A comprehensive reference for assessments in psychology, education, and business (2nd ed.).* Kansas City: Tests Corporation of America.

Vandeloo, M. C. (1977). "A study of coping behavior of runaway adolescents as related to situational stresses" (Doctoral dissertation, The Catholic University of America, 1977). *Dissertation Abstracts International,* 38, 2387.

Van-Houten, T. A. (1977). "Life stress: A predictor of adolescent running away" (Doctoral dissertation, The Catholic University of America, 1977). *Dissertation Abstracts International,* 38, 5719.

Walker, D. K. (1975). *Runaway youth: An annotated bibliography and literature review.* (ERIC Document Reproduction Service No. ED 138907).

Widiger, T. A. (1985). "Review of the Millon Adolescent Personality Inventory." In J. V. Mitchell, Jr. (Ed.). *Ninth Mental Measurements Yearbook* (pp. 979-981). Lincoln: The University of Nebraska Press.

Williams, A. D. (1977). "A comparison study of family dynamics and personality characteristics of runaways and non-runaways" (Doctoral dissertation, United States International University, 1977). *Dissertation Abstracts International, 39,* 5096B.

Wirt, R.D., Lachar, D., Klinedinst, J.K., & Seat, P.D. (1984). *Multidimensional Description of Child Personality: A manual for the Personality Inventory for Children.* Los Angeles: Western Psychological Services.

Index